The Cloud Upon The Sanctuary

by

Karl von Eckartshausen

Translated by
Isabel de Steiger

Introduction by
A. E. Waite

THE BOOK TREE
San Diego, California

This edition first published
1896
by
George Redway
London

ISBN 978-1-58509-277-2

Cover layout and design
by Toni Villalas

Published by
The Book Tree
P.O. Box 16476
San Diego, CA 92176
www.thebooktree.com

FOREWORD

This book is recognized as a classic of Christian mysticism and is highly recommended for those seeking a deeper spiritual sense of themselves and the Christian faith. Jesus is represented as the Wisdom of God, working in all things and always with us. Despite our fallen natures we are still able to reach into the wholeness and completeness that is offered. If we can find a way to work around our imperfections and reach deep within ourselves, there can be a true form of salvation. We must work in spiritual ways to access this hidden nature. That is what this book offers. Through meditative work and deeper awareness we are able to pierce the veil, or "cloud", and be able to experience our more divine natures. The author holds out hope that the principles within this book may one day allow people to live more spiritual lives, which in turn could bring more harmony and peace to the world. This book is a great tool that allows one to open up into the deeper, spiritual self.

Paul Tice

CONTENTS

INTRODUCTION

APART from "The Cloud upon the Sanctuary," Eckartshausen is a name only to the Christian Transcendentalists of England. He wrote much, and at his period and in his place, he exercised some considerable influence; but his other works are practically unknown among us, while in Germany the majority at least seem forgotten, even among the special class to which some of them might be assumed to appeal. "The Cloud upon the Sanctuary" has, I believe, always remained in the memory of a few, and is destined still to survive, for it carries with it a message of very deep significance to all those who look beneath the body of religious doctrine for the one principle of life which energizes the whole organism. This translation has offered it for the first time to English readers, and it enters here upon the third phase of its existence. It appeared originally in the pages of "The Unknown World," a magazine devoted to the deeper understanding of philosophical and mystical religion, and it was afterwards republished in volume form, of which edition this is a new issue. It has attracted very considerable attention and deserved it; it has even been translated into French, under the auspices of the late Countess of Caithness, for the pages of *L'Aurore*. These few words of bibliography are not unnecessary because they establish the fact that there has been some little sentiment of interest working within a restricted circle, as one may hope, towards a more general diffusion and knowledge of a document which is at once suggestive from the literary standpoint and profoundly moving from other and higher considerations. It encourages me to think that many persons who know and appreciate it now, or may come under its influence in the future, will learn with pleasure the little that I can tell them of its author, the Councillor Eckartshausen, and of certain other books not of his writing, which, as I think, connect therewith, and the study of which may help us to understand its message.

Perhaps the most interesting thing that I can say at the beginning concerning Eckartshausen is that he connects with that group of Theosophists of which Lavater was so important a figure, the Baron Kirchberger an accomplished and interesting recorder, and Louis Claude de Saint-Martin a correspondent in France and a certain source of leading. In his letters to Saint-Martin, Kirchberger says that Eckartshausen, with whom he was in frequent communication, was a man of immense reading and wonderful fertility; he regarded him in other respects as an extraordinary personage, "whatever way providence may have led him." It would appear that at this period, namely, in 1795, Eckartshausen was looking for and obtaining his chief light from the mystical study of numbers, but was also, to use the veiled and cautious language of the correspondence, in enjoyment of more direct favours. Saint-Martin confesses on his own part that he was more interested in Eckartshausen than he could express. Kirchberger must have held him in even higher estimation, and undertook a journey to the Swiss frontier actually for the purpose of receiving from him the personal communication of the Lost Word; but the illness of the proposed communicator frustrated this project. The point is important because it establishes the pretensions of Eckartshausen. As to the Councillor of Berne so to us, he comes speaking with authority; and whatever may be our opinion as to the kind of sacramentalism or economy which was conveyed in a proposal to communicate the incommunicable name, there are some of us who know, at least within certain limits, that the little book which I am here introducing is not one of vain pretension. Saint-Martin acknowledges that part of the numerical system of Eckartshausen was in astonishing agreement with things that he had learned long ago in his own school of initiation—that of Martines de Pasqually. Altogether the French mystic had formed the best opinion possible of his German brother, and his Swiss correspondent further tells us that Eckartshausen, although a courtier, walked in the narrow way of the inner life. In a letter to Kirchberger dated March 19th, 1795, Eckartshausen bears witness to his own personal experience and instructions received from above, his consciousness of a higher presence, the answers which he had received and the visions, with the steps by which he had advanced even to the attainment of what he terms "the Law in its fullness." I have thought it well to give these data derived from private correspondence, the publication of which was never designed or expected at the time, because they constitute a sketch of Eckartshausen taken to some extent unawares, when there could be the least reason to suppose that he was adopting an attitude. Let us now compare the very strong claim which they incorporate with that of "The Cloud upon the Sanctuary" itself, and the little analysis which I shall give here will, I think, be otherwise serviceable to readers as a summary of the chief purport of the work. It is possible by seeking inwardly to approach the essential wisdom, and this wisdom is Jesus Christ who is also the essence of love within us. The truth of this statement can be experimentally proved by any one, the condition of the experience being the awakening within us of a spiritual faculty cognizing spiritual objects as objectively and naturally as the outward senses perceive natural phenomenon. This organ is the intuitive sense of the transcendental world, and its awakening, which is the highest object of religion, takes place in three stages: (*a*) morally, by the way of inspiration; (*b*) intellectually, by the way of illumination; (*c*) spiritually, by the way of revelation. The awakening of this organ is the lifting of the cloud from the sanctuary, enabling our hearts to become receptive of God, even in this world. The knowledge of these mysteries has been always preserved by an advanced school, illuminated inwardly by the Saviour, and continued from the beginning of things to the present time. This community is the Invisible Celestial Church, founded immediately after the Fall, and receiving a first-hand revelation for the raising of humanity. But the weakness of men as they multiplied necessitated an external society, namely, the Outward Church, which, in the course of time, became separated from the Inner Church, also through human weakness. The external church was originally consecrated in Abraham, but received its highest perfection in the mystery of Jesus Christ. The Interior Church is invisible and yet governs all; it is perpetuated in silence but in real activity, "and united the science of the temple of the ancient alliance with the spirit of the Saviour," or of the interior alliance. This community of light is the reunion of all those capable of receiving light, and is known as the Communion of Saints. It possesses its school, its chair, its doctor, and a rule for students, with forms and objects of study, and in short a method by which they study, together with degrees for successive development to higher altitudes. We must not, however, regard it as a secret society, meeting at certain times, choosing its elders and members, and united by special objects; for even the chief does not invariably know all the members, and those who are ripe are joined to the general members when they thought least likely, and at a point of which they knew nothing. The society forms a theocratic republic, which one day will be the Regent-Mother of the whole world. Its members are exactly acquainted with the innermost of religions and of the Holy Mysteries, but these treasures are concealed in so simple a manner that they baffle unqualified research.

This doctrine of the interior church must be interpreted by everyone after his own lights; it is presented by Eckartshausen as one having full knowledge and ambassadorial powers, as one speaking from the centre. My purpose is solely to show that he was sincere, and this sincerity furnishes us with one more proof, out of many which are to be derived from other and independent sources, that there is a great experiment possible, and that some have performed it. The sincerity of which I speak is I think illustrated by his life, which I will now summarise briefly. Carl Von Eckartshausen was born on June 28th, 1752, at the Castle of Haimbhausen in Bavaria, and was the natural son of Count Carl of Haimbhausen by Marie Anne Eckhart, the daughter of the overseer of the estates. His mother died in giving birth to him, and he appears to have been the subject of the most solicitous affection on the part of his father, being educated with the utmost pains. However, from the earliest years, his illegitimacy is said to have filled him with perpetual melancholy and an inclination to retire from the world, characteristics which at the same time endeared him to his family and friends. Through all his life he remained less or more a prey to the painful consequences of his original disqualification. He was destined notwithstanding to a career of some public importance. His first education was received at the college of Munich, and he afterwards proceeded to Ingoldsladt for the study of philosophy and law, which he pursued with marked success. His university course at an end, his father procured him the title of Aulic Councillor; and in 1780 he was appointed censor of the library at Munich. This, in spite of the rectitude and goodness which characterised him, made him many enemies, but the favour of the Elector Carl Theodore sustained him against all combinations. In 1784 he was nominated Keeper of the Archives of the Electoral House, an appointment said to have been conferred upon him through the desire of the Elector to keep him near his person. He published in all some sixty-nine works, embracing many classes of literature, including science, the fine arts, the drama, politics, religion, history, and, in particular, certain contributions of great merit to the occult sciences. As already indicated, the majority of these are now forgotten, though some of his plays seem to have been successful in their day. "The Prejudice of Birth" in particular, his first published drama, is described as abounding in felicitous situations and interest. He even attempted a comedy, and this also received considerable approbation. One only of his books, under the title "God is the Purest Love," commanded wide popularity. Sixty editions are said to have been published in Germany, and it was translated into most languages of Europe, as well as into Latin. It is a small collection of Catholic prayers and meditations on the fear of God, the love of God, the elevation of man's sentiments towards his Creator, the knowledge of the Eternal, etc. There are also devotional exercises for use at Mass, before and after Confession, and at Communion, with acts of penance and adoration to the Blessed Virgin. In a word, I fail to see wherein or how far it differs from the innumerable manuels of piety which have been produced during the last two or three centuries for the use of the Catholic laity. I believe, however, that it still circulates in Germany, and perhaps even in France; it is said to have a wonderful charm, though its intense mysticism is also stated to have puzzled some of its admirers; it has indeed been described as speaking the language and expressing the soul of Fenelon. Eckartshausen, however, as already indicated, wrote other and very different books, some on magic and some on the properties of numbers, and he is even accredited with a certain knowledge of Alchemy. Finally, he was the author of "The Cloud upon the Sanctuary," though the biographers to whom I am indebted almost for the words of this notice have scarcely mentioned this last and crowning production of his intellectual life. In his private capacity he was exceedingly amiable and charitable, devoting every month the result of his economies to the poor, and his whole time to the practice of virtue. He was married three times, and left several children. He died on May 13th, 1813, after a painful illness. The monographs of his period mention him as one of the best writers of Bavaria.

There are two matters to which before concluding I wish to draw attention briefly, and, as regards the first, in a very particular manner. The point of view from which "The Cloud upon the Sanctuary" should be regarded is important from the claim which it makes. What is this inner church of which Eckartshausen speaks, is a question which readers must answer for themselves, according to their best direction. One thing which it is not has been indicated by Eckartshausen himself. It is not any corporate body existing merely within the church and controlling and leading it from a specific local centre. This possibility being negatived by the best of all authority on the subject, I should like on my own responsibility to negative also its most direct and clearest antithesis. It does not answer to the collective mind or oversoul of the most advanced members of the visible church, nor is it the *consensus omnium sanctorum* which, according to the old church maxim, is *sensus spiritus sancti.* Despite the absence of all corporate bonds, there is in the claim itself too direct a suggestion of conscious association occurring somehow in this present physical life. We must take the key which Eckartshausen himself offers, namely, that there is within all of us a dormant faculty, the awakening of which within us gives entrance, as it develops, into a new world of consciousness, which is one of the initial stages of that state which he, in common with all other mystics, terms union with the Divine. In that union, outside all formal sects, all orthodox bonds of fellowship and veils and webs of symbolism, we shall form or do form actually a great congregation, the first fruits of immortality, and in virtue of the solidarity of humanity, and in virtue of the great doctrine of the communication of all things holy with all that seeks for holiness, the above and the below, this congregation is, in very truth, the leader of the visible church of faith, aspiration and struggle, the church triumphant over-watching the church militant, and the channel through which the graces and the benedictions of the holy and glorious Zion are administered to the Zion which is on earth.

The second point concerns certain books which I have promised to mention as connecting with the claim of Eckartshausen, and perhaps in some measure assisting us to get in touch with that claim. Unfortunately, in this restricted notice, I can do little more than name them. The first is "The Mystery of the Cross," originally published in 1732, anonymously, in the French language, but evidently written by a foreigner. It is a profound and beautiful work which, unknown to the world at large, has in private, if I may so speak, influenced many to their advancement, and to the deeper understanding and fruition of the hidden truth. Strongly embedded in this book will be found several of the governing ideas and aspirations of schools of mystic thought which became illustrious in later years. I may add that I am acquainted with the existence of a translation made many years ago, but still remaining in manuscript. The next books which I would note come at first sight a little strangely in the professed connection, but they enter none the less into the series; they are the two dramatic poems of the German poet, Werner, namely, "The Templars in Cyprus" and "The Brothers of the Cross." They are the work of a man who was intimately acquainted with the occult movement of his period—that of the French Revolution—and a participant therein. After all his experience he carried his great genius and exceptional knowledge into the fold of the Latin Church and became a priest. His two plays convey many moving suggestions of a guiding but unknown hand leading the Christian Church. The next book is of Russian origin, but was translated into French and published in Paris in 1801; of this translation a reprint was issued recently at Lyons. It is entitled "Some Characteristics of the Interior Church." It connects the point of view which is met with in "The Mystery of the Cross" with that of Eckartshausen, and is interesting on account of its origin, and also for certain Martinistic associations, but it is less suggestive and less profound. Finally, there is a very remarkable and I may add a very rare series of works published at Berleburg in the province of Westphalia in seven volumes, dated 1738. It is entitled "New Spiritual Discourses on various matters of the Interior Life and the Doctrines of the Christian Religion, or testimony of a Child of Truth concerning the Ways of the Spirit." These discourses occupy three volumes; two others contain a commentary on the Apocalypse; the sixth volume is a literal and mystical explanation of the epistle to the Romans, with some supplementary papers and a catechism of the science of Christian religion. The seventh volume is another commentary, verse for verse, on the first three chapters of Genesis. The collection as a whole may perhaps be best described as an appeal from external creeds with their differences, their arguments and their justifications, to the witness of the heart itself. It is an appeal also to the mystical doctors of the church, and it cites many of the great mystics from Tauler and Ruysbroek to Engelbrecht, Antoinette de Bourignon and Madame de Guyon. The discourses on the union of the Church of Christ and the spiritual union of the children of God, as also on a new church, in the second volume, will be found very interesting to students of Eckartshausen. There are also extraordinary analogies with Saint-Martin, Eckartshausen and the "Mystery of the Cross" to be found in the third volume, and having regard to the proximity of the date of publication to that of the last work, I incline to the opinion that there may have been some connection also in the authorship. When all these works have been studied, not in the letter but in the spirit, along with "The Cloud upon the Sanctuary," the spiritual truths which Eckartshausen has to some extent veiled, and his motives for doing so, will not be beyond discernment, nor the line of his experiences in all cases beyond pursuit. I should add that, so far as I can trace, Eckartshausen always remained in loyal communication with the external church in which he was originally trained, and did not therefore regard apostasy and rebellion as among the first evidences of personal illumination. Perhaps, like one of the Eastern teachers, he thought that some things could be changed from within, and essentially, without altering outward names and forms.

A. E. WAITE.

THE CLOUD UPON THE SANCTUARY

LETTER I

THERE is no age more remarkable to the quiet observer than our own. Everywhere there is a fermentation in the minds of men; everywhere there is a battle between light and darkness, between exploded thought and living ideas, between powerless wills and living active force; in short everywhere is there war between animal man and growing spiritual man.

It is said that we live in an age of light, but it would be truer to say that we are living in an age of twilight; here and there a luminous ray pierces through the mists of darkness, but does not light to full clearness either our reason or our hearts. Men are not of one mind, scientists dispute, and where there is discord, truth is not yet apprehended.

The most important objects for humanity are still undetermined. No one is agreed either on the principle of rationality or on the principle of morality, or on the cause of the will. This proves that though we are dwelling in an age of light, we do not well understand what emanates from our hearts—and what from our heads. Probably we should have this information much sooner if we did not imagine that we have the light of knowledge already in our hands, or if we would cast a look on our weakness, and recognise that we require a more brilliant illumination. We live in the times of idolatry of the intellect, we place a common torchlight upon the altar and we loudly proclaim the aurora, that now daylight is really about to appear, and that the world is emerging more and more out of obscurity into the full day of perfection, through the arts, sciences, cultured taste, and even from a purer understanding of religion.

Poor mankind! To what standpoint have you raised the happiness of man? Has there ever been an age which has counted so many victims to humanity as the present? Has there ever been an age in which immorality and egotism have been greater or more dominant than in this one? The tree is known by its fruits. Mad men! With your imaginary natural reason, from whence have you the light by which you are so willing to enlighten others? Are not all your ideas borrowed from your senses which do not give you the reality but merely its phenomena? Is it not true that in time and space all knowledge is but relative? Is it not true that all which we call reality is but relative, for absolute truth is not to be found in the phenomenal world. Thus your natural reason does not possess its true essence, but only the appearance of truth and light; and the more this appearance increases and spreads, the more the *essence of light* inwardly fades, and the man confuses himself with this appearance and gropes vainly after the dazzling phantasmal images he conjures.

The philosophy of our age raises the natural intellect into independent objectivity, and gives it judicial power, she exempts it from any superior authority, she makes it voluntary, converting it into divinity by closing all harmony and communication with God; and this god Reason, which has no other law but its own, is to govern Man and make him happy! . . .

. . . Darkness able to spread light! . . . Death capable of giving Life! . . .

The truth leads man to happiness. Can you give it?

That which you call truth is a form of conception empty of real matter, the knowledge of which is acquired from without and through the senses, and the understanding co-ordinates them by observed synthetic relationship into science or opinion.

You abstract from the Scriptures and Tradition their moral, theoretical and practical truth; but as individuality is the principle of your intelligence, and as egotism is the incentive to your will, you do not see, by your light, the moral law which dominates, or you repel it with your will. It is to this length that the light of to-day has penetrated. Individuality under the cloak of false philosophy is a child of corruption.

Who can pretend that the sun is in full zenith if no bright rays illuminate the earth, and no warmth vitalises vegetation? If wisdom does not benefit man, if love does not make him happy, but very little has been done for him on the whole.

Oh! if only natural man, that is, sensuous man, would only learn to see that the source of his intelligence and the incentive of his will are only his individuality, he would then seek interiorly for a higher source, and he would thereby approach that which alone can give this true element, because it is *wisdom in its essential substance.*

Jesus Christ is that Wisdom, Truth, and Love. He, as Wisdom, is the Principle of reason, and the Source of the purest intelligence. As Love, He is the Principle of morality, the true and pure incentive of the will.

Love and Wisdom beget the spirit of truth, interior light; this light illuminates us and makes supernatural things objective to us.

It is inconceivable to what depths of error a man falls when he abandons simple truths of faith by opposing his own opinions.

Our century tries to decide by its (brain) intelligence, wherein lies the principle or ground of reason and morality, or the ground of the will; if the scientists were mindful, they would see that these things are better answered in the heart of the simplest man, than through their most brilliant casuistry. The practical Christian finds this incentive to the will, the principle of all morality, really and objectively in his heart; and this incentive is expressed in the following formula:—"Love God with all thy heart, and thy neighbour as thyself."

The love of God and his neighbour is the motive for the Christian's will, and the essence of love itself is Jesus Christ *in us.*

It is in this way the principle of reason is wisdom in us; and the essence of wisdom, wisdom in its substance, is again Jesus Christ, the light of the world. Thus we find in Him the principle of reason and of morality.

All that I am now saying is not hyperphysical extravagance; it is reality, absolute truth, that everyone can prove for himself by experience, as soon as he receives in himself the principle of all reason and morality—Jesus Christ, being wisdom and love *in essence.*

But the eye of the man of sensuous perception only is firmly closed to the fundamental basis of all that is true and to all that is transcendental.

The intelligence which many would fain raise to legislative authority is only that of the senses, whose light differs from that of transcendental reason, as does the phosphorescent glimmer of decayed wood from the glories of sunshine.

Absolute truth does not exist for sensuous man;

it exists only for interior and spiritual man who possesses a suitable sensorium; or, to speak more correctly, who possesses an interior sense to receive the absolute truth of the transcendental world, a spiritual faculty which cognises spiritual objects as objectively and naturally as the exterior senses perceive external phenomena.

This interior faculty of the man spiritual, this sensorium for the metaphysical world, is unfortunately not known to those who cognise only outside of it—for it is a mystery of the kingdom of God.

The current incredulity towards everything which is not cognised objectively by our senses is the explanation for the misconception of truths which are, of all, most important to man.

But how can this be otherwise? In order to see one must have eyes, to hear, one must have ears. Every apparent object requires its appropriate senses. So it is that transcendental objects require their sensorium—and this said sensorium is closed in most men. Hence men judge the metaphysical world through the intelligence of their senses, even as the blind imagine colours and the deaf judge tones—without suitable senses.

There is an objective and substantial ground of reason, an objective and substantial motive for the will. These two together form the new principle *of life*, and morality is there essentially inherent. This pure substance of reason and will, re-uniting in us the divine and the human, is Jesus Christ, the light of the world, who must enter into direct relationship with us, to be really recognized.

This real knowledge is actual faith, in which everything takes place in spirit and in truth.

Thus one ought to have a sensorium fitted for this communication, an organised spiritual sensorium, a spiritual and interior faculty able to receive this light; but it is closed to most men by their senses.

This interior organ is the intuitive sense of the transcendental world, and until this intuitive sense is effective in us we can have no certainty of more lofty truths.

This organism is naturally inactive since the Fall, which degraded man to the world of physical senses alone. The gross matter which envelops this interior sensorium is a film which veils the internal eye, and therefore prevents the exterior eye from seeing into spiritual realms. This same matter muffles our internal hearing, so that we are deaf to the sounds of the metaphysical world; it so paralyses our spiritual speech that we can scarcely stammer words of sacred import, *words we fully pronounced once*, and by virtue of which we held authority over the elements and the external world.

The opening of this spiritual sensorium is the mystery of the New Man—the mystery of Regeneration, and of the vital union between God and man—it is the noblest object of religion on earth, that religion whose sublime goal is none other than to unite men with God in Spirit and in Truth.

We can therefore easily see by this how it is that religion tends always towards the subjection of the senses. It does so because it desires to make the spiritual man dominant, in order that the spiritual or truly rational man may govern the man of sense. Philosophy feels this truth, only its error consists in not apprehending the true source of reason, and because she would replace it by individuality by sensuous reason.

As man has internally a spiritual organ and a sensorium to receive the true principle of divine wisdom, or a true motive for the will or divine love, he has also exteriorly a physical and material sensorium to receive the *appearance* of light and truth. As external nature can have no absolute truth, but only phenomenally relative, therefore, human reason cannot cognise pure truth, it can but apprehend through the appearance of phenomena, which excites the lust of the eye, and in this as a source of action consists the corruption of sensuous man and the degradation of nature.

This exterior sensorium in man is composed of frail matter, whereas the internal sensorium is organized fundamentally from incorruptible, transcendental, and metaphysical substance.

The first is the cause of our depravity and our mortality, the second the cause of our incorruptibility and of our immortality.

In the regions of material and corruptible nature mortality hides immortality, therefore all our trouble results from corruptible mortal matter. In order that man should be released from this distress, it is necessary that the immortal and incorruptible principle, which dwells within, should expand and absorb the corruptible principle, so that the envelope of the senses should be opened, and man appear in his pristine purity.

This natural envelope is a truly corruptible substance found in our blood, forming the fleshly bonds binding our immortal spirits under the servitude of the mortal flesh.

This envelope can be rent more or less in every man, and this places him in greater spiritual liberty, and makes him more cognisant of the transcendental world.

There are three different degrees in the opening of our spiritual sensorium.

The first degree reaches to the moral plane only, the transcendental world energises through us in but by interior action, called inspiration.

The second and higher degree opens this sensorium to the reception of the spiritual and the intellectual, and the metaphysical world *works* in us by interior *illumination*.

The third degree, which is the highest and most seldom attained, opens the whole inner man. It breaks the crust which fills our spiritual eyes and ears; it reveals the kingdom of spirit, and enables us to see objectively, metaphysical, and transcendental sights; hence all visions are explained fundamentally.

Thus we have an internal sense of objectivity as well as externally. Only the objects and the senses are different. Exteriorly animal and sensual motives act in us and corruptible sensuous matter energises. Interiorly it is metaphysical and indivisible substance which gains admittance within, and the incorruptible and immortal essence of our Spirit receives its influence. Nevertheless, generally things pass much in the same way interiorly as they do externally. The law is everywhere the same. Hence, as the spirit or our internal man has quite other senses, and quite another objective sight from the rational man; one need not be surprised that it (the spirit) should remain an enigma for the scientists of our age, for those who have no objective sense of the transcendental and spiritual world. Hence they measure the supernatural by the measurement of the senses. However, we owe a debt of gratitude towards the philosopher Kant for his view of the truths we have promulgated.

Kant has shown incontestably that the natural reason can know absolutely nothing of what is supernatural, and that it can never understand analytically or synthetically, neither can it prove the possibility of the reality of Love, Spirit, or of the Deity.

This is a great truth, lofty and beneficial for our

epoch, though it is true that St Paul has already enunciated it (1 Cor. i. 2-24). But the Pagan philosophy of Christian scientists has been able to overlook it up to Kant. The virtue of this truth is double. First, it puts insurmountable limits to the sentiment, to the fanaticism and to the extravagance of carnal reason. Then it shows by dazzling contrast the necessity and divinity of Revelation. It proves that our human reason, in its state of unfoldment, *has no other* objective source for the supernatural than revelation, the only source of instruction in Divine things or of the spiritual world, the soul and its immortality; hence it follows that without revelation it is absolutely impossible to suppose or conjecture anything regarding these matters.

We are, therefore, indebted to Kant for proving philosophically now-a-days, what long ago was taught in a more advanced and illuminated school, *that without revelation no knowledge of God, neither any doctrine touching the soul, could be at all possible.*

It is therefore clear that a universal Revelation must serve as a fundamental basis to all mundane religion.

Hence, following Kant, it is clear that the transmundane knowledge is wholly inaccessible to natural reason, and that God inhabits a world of light, into which no speculation of the unfolded reason can penetrate. Thus the rational man, or man of human reason, has no sense of transcendental reality, and therefore it was necessary that it should be *revealed* to him, for which faith is required, because the means are given to him by faith whereby his inner sensorium unfolds, and through which he can apprehend the reality of truths otherwise incapable of being understood by the natural man.

It is quite true that with new senses we can acquire sense of further reality. This reality exists already, but is not known to us, because we lack the organ by which to cognise it. One must not lay the fault to the percept, but on the receptive organ.

With, however, the development of the new organ we have a new perception, a sense of new reality. Without it the spiritual world cannot exist for us, because the organ rendering it objective to us is not developed.

With, however, its unfoldment, the curtain is all at once raised, the impenetrable veil is torn away, the cloud before the Sanctuary lifts, a new world suddenly exists for us, scales fall from the eyes, and we are at once transported from the phenomenal world to the regions of truth.

God alone is *substance*, absolute truth ; He alone is He who *is*, and we are what He has made us. For Him, all exists in Unity ; for us, all exists in multiplicity.

A great many men have no more idea of the development of the inner sensorium than they have of the true and objective life of the spirit, which they neither perceive nor foresee in any manner. Hence it is impossible to them to know that one can comprehend the spiritual and transcendental, and that one can be raised to the supernatural, even to vision.

The great and true work of building the Temple consists solely in destroying the miserable Adamic hut and in erecting a divine temple; this means, in other words, to develop in us the interior sensorium, or the organ to receive God. After this process, the metaphysical and incorruptible principle rules over the terrestrial, and man begins to live, not any longer in the principle of self-love, but in the Spirit and in the Truth, of which he is the Temple.

The moral law then evolves into love for one's neighbour in deed and in truth, whereas for the natural man it is but a simple attitude of thought; and the spiritual man, regenerated in spirit, sees all *in its essence*, of which the natural man has only the forms void of thought, mere empty sounds, symbols and letters, which are all dead images without interior spirit. The lofty aim of religion is the intimate union of man with God; and this union is possible in this world; but it only can be by the opening of our inner sensorium, which enables our hearts to become receptive to God.

Therein are mysteries that our philosophy does not dream of, the key to which is not to be found in scholastic science.

Meanwhile, a more advanced school has always

existed to whom this deposition of all science has been confided, and this school was the community illuminated interiorly by the Saviour, the society of the Elect, which has continued from the first day of creation to the present time; its members, it is true, are scattered all over the world, but they have always been united in the spirit and in one truth; they have had but one intelligence and one source of truth, but one doctor and one master; but in whom resides substantially the whole plenitude of God, and who alone initiates them into the high mysteries of Nature and the Spiritual World.

This community of light has been called from all time the invisible celestial Church, or the most ancient of all communities, of which we will speak more fully in our next letter.

LETTER II

It is necessary, my dear brothers in the Lord, to give you a clear idea of the interior Church; of that illuminated Community of God which is scattered throughout the world, but which is governed by one truth and united in one spirit.

This enlightened community has existed since the first day of the world's creation, and its duration will be to the last day of time.

This community possesses a School, in which all who thirst for knowledge are instructed by the Spirit of Wisdom itself; and all the mysteries of God and of nature are preserved in this School for the children of light. . . . Perfect knowledge of God, of nature, and of humanity are the objects of instruction in this school. It is from her that all truths penetrate into the world, she is the School of the Prophets, and of all who search for wisdom, and it is in this community alone that truth and the explanation of all mystery is to be found. It is the most hidden of communities yet possesses members from many circles; of such is this School. From all time there has been an exterior school based on the interior one, of which it is but the outer expression. From all time, therefore, there has been a hidden assembly, a society of the Elect, of those who sought for and had capacity for light, and this interior society was called the interior Sanctuary or Church. All that the external Church possesses in symbol ceremony or rite is the letter expressive outwardly of the spirit of truth residing in the interior Sanctuary.

Hence this Sanctuary composed of scattered members, but tied by the bonds of perfect unity and love, has been occupied from the earliest ages in building the grand Temple through the regeneration of humanity, by which the reign of God will be manifest. This society is in the communion of those who have most capacity for light, *i.e.*, the Elect. The Elect are united in truth, and their Chief is the Light of the World himself, Jesus Christ, the One Anointed in light, the single mediator for the human race, the Way, the Truth, and the Life —Primitive light, wisdom, and the only *medium* by which man can return to God.

The interior Church was formed immediately after the fall of man, and received from God at first-hand the revelation of the means by which fallen humanity could be again raised to its rights and delivered from its misery. It received the primitive charge of all revelation and mystery; it received the key of true science, both divine and natural.

But when men multiplied, the frailty of man and his weakness necessitated an exterior society which veiled the interior one, and concealed the spirit and the truth in the letter. Because many people were not capable of comprehending great interior truth, and the danger would have been too great in confiding the most Holy to incapable people. Therefore, interior truths were wrapped in external and perceptible ceremonies, so that men, by the perception of the outer, which is the symbol of the interior, might by degrees be enabled safely to approach the interior spiritual truths.

But the inner truth has always been confided to him who in his day had the most capacity for illumination, and he became the sole guardian of the original Trust, as High Priest of the Sanctuary.

When it became necessary that interior truths should be enfolded in exterior ceremony and symbol, on account of the real weakness of men who were not capable of bearing the Light of Light, then exterior worship began. It was, however, always the type and symbol of the interior, that is to say, the symbol of the true homage offered to God *in spirit* and *in truth.*

The difference between spiritual and animal man, and between rational and sensual man, made the exterior and interior imperative. Interior truth passed into the external wrapped in symbol and ceremony, so that sensuous man could observe, and be gradually thereby led to interior truth. Hence external worship was symbolically typical of interior truths, and of the true relationship between man and God before and after the Fall, and of his most perfect reconciliation. All the symbols of external worship are based upon the three fundamental relations—the Fall, the Reconciliation, and the Complete Atonement.

The care of the external service was the occupation of priests, and every father of a family was in the ancient times charged with this duty. First fruits and the first born among animals were offered to God, symbolizing that all that preserves and nourishes us comes from Him; also that animal man must be killed to make room for rational and spiritual man.

The external worship of God would never have been separated from interior service but for the weakness of man which tends too easily to forget the spirit in the letter, but the spirit of God is vigilant to note in every nation those who are able to receive light, and they are employed as agents to spread the light according to man's capacity, and to revivify the dead letter.

Through these divine instruments the interior truths of the Sanctuary were taken into every nation, and modified symbolically according to their customs, capacity for instruction, climate, and receptiveness. So that the external types of every religion, worship, ceremonies and Sacred Books in general have more or less clearly, as their object of instruction, the interior truths of the Sanctuary, by which man, but only in the latter days, will be conducted to the universal knowledge of the one Absolute Truth.

The more the external worship of a people has remained united with the spirit of esoteric truth, the purer its religion; but the wider the difference between the symbolic letter and the invisible truth, the more imperfect has become the religion; even so far among some nations as to degenerate into polytheism. Then the external form entirely parted from its inner truth, when ceremonial observances without soul or life remained alone.

When the *germs* of the most important truths had been carried everywhere by God's agents, He chose a certain people to raise up *a vital symbol* destined by Him to manifest forth the means by which He intended to govern the human race in its present condition, and by which it would be raised into complete purification and perfection.

God Himself communicated to this people its exterior religious legislation, He gave all the symbols and enacted all the ceremonies, and they contained the impress, as it were, of the great esoteric truth of the Sanctuary.

God consecrated this external Church in Abraham, gave commandments through Moses, and it received its highest perfection in the double message of Jesus Christ, existing personally in poverty and suffering, and by the communication of His Spirit in the glory of the Resurrection.

Now, as God Himself laid the foundation of the

external Church, the whole of the symbols of external worship formed the science of the Temple and of the Priests in those days, because the mysteries of the most sacred truths became external through revelation alone. The scientific acquaintance of this holy symbolism was the science to unite fallen man once more with God, hence religion received its name from being the science of rebinding man with God, to bring man back to his origin.

One sees plainly by this pure idea of religion in general that unity in religion is within the inner Sanctuary, and that the multiplicity of external religions can never alter the true unity which is at the base of every exterior.

The wisdom of the ancient temple alliance was preserved by priests and by prophets.

To the priests was confided the external,—the letter of the symbol, hieroglyphics. The prophets had the charge of the inner truth, and their occupation was to continually recall the priest to the spirit in the letter, when inclined to lose it. The science of the priests was that of the knowledge of exterior symbol.

That of the prophets was experimental possession of the truth of the symbols. In the interior the spirit lived. There was, therefore, in the ancient alliance a school of prophets and of priests, the one occupying itself with the spirit in the emblem, the other with the emblem itself. The priests had the external possession of the Ark, of the shewbread, of the candlesticks, of the manna, of Aaron's rod, and the prophets were in interior possession of the inner spiritual truth which was represented exteriorly by the symbols just mentioned.

The external Church of the ancient alliance was visible, the interior Church was always invisible, must be invisible, and yet must govern all, because force and power are alone confided to her.

When the divine external * worship abandoned the interior worship, it fell, and God proved by a remarkable chain of circumstances that the letter could not exist without the spirit, that it is only there to lead to the spirit, and it is useless and even rejected by God if it fails in its object.

As the spirit of nature extends to the most sterile depths to vivify and preserve and cause growth in everything susceptible to its influence, likewise the spirit of light spreads itself interiorly among nations to animate everywhere the dead letter by the living spirit.

This is why we find a Job among idolators, a Melchizedek among strange nations, a Joseph with the Egyptian priests, a Moses in the country of Midian, as living proofs the interior community of those who are capable of receiving light was united

* I can't but think here that the words interior and exterior are transposed in translating from the original German to the French from which I translate it, but I put it as I find in the text of the very valuable edition to which I have access.—I. de S.

by one spirit and one truth in all times and in all nations.

To these agents of light from the one inner community was united the Chief of all agents, Jesus Christ Himself, in the midst of time as *royal priest* after the order of Melchizedek.

The divine agents of the ancient alliance hitherto represented only specialised perfections of God; therefore a powerful movement was required which should show all at once—*all in one*. A universal type appeared, which gave the real touch of perfect unity to the picture, which opened a fresh door, and destroyed the number of the slavery of humanity.

The law of love began when the image emanating from wisdom itself showed to man all the greatness of his being, vivified him anew, assured him of his immortality, and raised his intellectual status to that of being the true temple for the spirit.

This Chief Agent of all, this Saviour of the World and universal Regenerator, claimed man's whole attention to the primitive truth, whereby he can preserve his existence and recover his former dignity. Through the conditions of His own abasement He laid the base of the redemption of man, and He promised to accomplish it completely one day through His Spirit. He showed also truly in part among His apostles all that should come to pass in the future to all the Elect.

He linked the chain of the community of light among the Elect, to whom He sent the spirit of truth, and confided to them the true primitive instruction in all divine and natural things, as a sign that He would never forsake His community.

When the letter and symbolic worship of the external Church of the ancient alliance had been realised by the Incarnation of the Saviour, and verified in His person, new symbols became requisite for external use, which showed us through the letter the future accomplishment of universal redemption.

The rites and symbols of the external Christian Church were formed after the pattern of these unchangeable and fundamental truths, announcing things of a strength and of an importance impossible to describe, and revealed only to those who knew the innermost Sanctuary.

This Sanctuary remains changeless, though external religion receives in the course of time and circumstances varied modification, entailing separation from the interior spirit which can alone preserve the letter. The profane idea of wishing to "secularize" all that is Christian, and to Christianise all that is political, changed the exterior edifice, and covered with the shadow of death all that was interior light and life. Hence divisions and heresies, and the spirit of Sophistry ready to expound the letter when it had already lost the essence of truth.

Current incredulity increased corruption to its utmost point, attacking the edifice of Christianity in its fundamental parts, and the sacred interior was mingled with the exterior, already enfeebled by the ignorance of weak man.

Then was born Deism; this brought forth materialism, which looked on the union of man with superior forces as imaginary; then finally came forth, partly from the head and partly from the heart, the last degree of man's degradation—Atheism.

In the midst of all this, truth reposes inviolable in the inner Sanctuary.

Faithful to the spirit of truth, which promised never to abandon its community, the members of the interior Church lived in silence, but in real activity, and united the science of the temple of the ancient alliance with the spirit of the great saviour of man—the spirit of the interior alliance, waiting humbly the great moment when the Lord will call them, and will assemble his community in order to give every dead letter external force and life.

This interior community of light is the reunion of all those capable of receiving light as Elect, and it is known as the *Communion of Saints*. The primitive receptacle for all strength and truth, confided to it from all time—it alone, says St Paul, is in the possession of the science of the Saints.

By it the agents of God were formed in every age, passing from the interior to the exterior, and communicating spirit and life to the dead letter as already said.

This illuminated community has been through

time the true school of God's spirit, and considered as school, it has its Chair, its Doctor, it possesses a rule for students, it has forms and objects for study, and, in short, a method by which they study.

It has, also, its degrees for successive development to higher altitudes.

The first and lowest degree consists in the moral good, by which the single will, subordinated to God, is led to God by the pure motive of willing with and to Jesus Christ, which it does through faith. The means by which the spirit of this school acts are called inspirations.

The second degree consists in the rational intellectuality, by which the understanding of the man of virtue, who is united to God, is crowned with wisdom and the light of knowledge, and the means which the spirit uses to produce this is called interior illumination.

The third and highest degree is the entire opening of our inner sensorium, by which the inner man perceives objectively and really, metaphysical verities. This is the highest degree when faith passes into open vision, and the means the spirit uses for this are real visions.

These are the three degrees of the school for true interior wisdom—that of the illuminated Society. The same spirit which ripens men for this community also distributes its degrees by the co-action of the ripened subject.

This school of wisdom has been forever most

secretly hidden from the world, because it is invisible and submissive solely to divine government.

It has never been exposed to the accidents of time and to the weakness of man. Because only the most capable were chosen for it, and the spirits who selected made no error.

Through this school were developed the germs of all the sublime sciences, which were first received by external schools, then clothed in other forms, and hence degenerating.

This society of sages communicated, according to time and circumstances, unto the exterior societies their symbolic hieroglyphs, in order to attract man to the great truths of their interior.

But all exterior societies subsist through this interior one giving them its spirit. As soon as external societies wish to be independent of the interior one, and to transform a temple of wisdom into a political edifice, the interior society retires and leaves only the letter without the spirit. It is thus that secret external societies of wisdom were nothing but hieroglyphic screens, the truth remaining inviolable in the sanctuary so that she might never be profaned.

In this interior society man finds wisdom and with her—*All*—not the wisdom of this world which is but scientific knowledge, which revolves round the outside but never touches the centre (in which is contained all strength), but true wisdom and men obeying her.

All disputes, all controversies, all the things belonging to the false cares of this world, fruitless discussions, useless germs of opinions which spread the seeds of disunion, all error, schisms, and systems are banished. Neither calumny nor scandal are known. Every man is honoured. Satire, that spirit which loves to make its neighbour smart, is unknown. Love alone reigns.

Want and feebleness are protected, and rejoicings are made at the elevation and greatness which man acquires.

We must not, however, imagine this society resembles any secret society, meeting at certain times, choosing its leaders and members, united by special objects. All societies, be what they may, can but come after this interior illuminated circle. This society knows none of the formalities which belong to the outer rings, the work of man. In this kingdom of power all outward forms cease.

God himself is the Power always present. The best man of his times, the chief himself, does not always know all the members, but the moment when it is the Will of God that he should accomplish any object, he finds them in the world with certainty to work for that purpose.

This community has no outside barriers. He who may be chosen by God is as the first, he presents himself among the others without presumption, and he is received by the others without jealousy.

If it be necessary that real members should meet together, they find and recognise each other with perfect certainty.

No disguise can be used, neither hypocrisy nor dissimulation could hide the characteristic qualities of this society, they are too genuine. All illusion is gone, and things appear in their true form.

No one member can choose another, unanimous choice is required. All men are called, the called may be chosen, if they become ripe for entrance.

Any one can look for the entrance, and any man who is within can teach another to seek for it; but only he who is fit can arrive inside.

Unprepared men occasion disorder in a community, and disorder is not compatible with the Sanctuary. This thrusts out all who are not homogeneous.

Worldly intelligence seeks this Sanctuary in vain, fruitless also will be the efforts of malice to penetrate these great mysteries; all is undecipherable to him who is not ripe, he can see nothing, read nothing in the interior.

He who is ripe is joined to the chain, perhaps often where he thought least likely, and at a point of which he knew nothing himself.

Seeking to become ripe, should be effort of him who sees wisdom.

But there are methods by which ripeness is attained, for in this holy communion is the primitive storehouse of the most ancient and original science of the human race, with the primitive mysteries also of all science. It is the unique and really illuminated community which is absolutely in possession of the key to all mystery, which knows the centre and source of all nature and creation. It is a society which unites superior strength to its own, and counts its members from more than one world. It is the society whose members form a theocratic republic, which one day will be the Regent Mother of the whole World.*

* Capitals are rarely employed. I always quote them, but occasionally use them in other places when the sense requires them, so as not to confuse the cases and genders, for instance, esprit evidently requires to be written occasionally Spirit, not spirit.

LETTER III

THE absolute truth lying in the centre of Mystery is like the sun, it blinds ordinary sight and man sees only the shadow. The eagle alone can gaze at the dazzling light, likewise only the prepared soul can bear its lustre. Nevertheless the great *Something* which is the inmost of the Holy Mysteries has never been hidden from the piercing gaze of him who can bear the light.

God and nature have no mysteries for their children. They are caused by the weakness of our nature, unable to support light, because it is not yet organised to bear the chaste light of unveiled truth.

This weakness is the Cloud that covers the Sanctuary; this is the curtain which veils the Holy of Holies.

But in order that man may recover the veiled light, strength and dignity, Divinity bends to the weakness of its creatures, and writes the truth that is interior and eternal mystery on the *outside of things*, so that man can transport himself through this to their spirit.

These letters are the ceremonies or the rituals of religion, which lead man to the interior life of union with God.

Mystic hieroglyphs are these letters also; they are sketches and designs holding interior and holy truth.

Religion and the Mysteries go hand in hand to lead our brethren to truth, both have for object the reversing and renewing of our natures, both have for the end the re-building of a temple inhabited by Wisdom and Love, or God with man.

But religion and the Mysteries would be useless phenomena if Divinity had not also accorded means to attain these great ends.

But these means are only in the innermost of the sanctuary. The Mysteries are required to build a temple to Religion, and religion is required to unite Man with God.

Such is the greatness of religion, and such the exalted dignity of the Mysteries from all time.

It would be unjust to you, beloved brothers, that we should think that you have *never* regarded the Holy Mysteries in this *real* aspect, the one which shows them as the only means able to preserve in purity and integrity the doctrine of the important truths concerning God, nature, and man. This doctrine was couched in holy symbolic language, and the truths which it contained having been gradually translated among the outer circle into the ordinary languages of man, became in consequence more obscure and unintelligible.

The Mysteries, as you know, beloved brothers, promise things which are and which will remain always the heritage of but a small number of men; these are the mysteries which can neither be bought nor sold publicly, and can only be acquired by a heart which has attained to wisdom and love.

He in whom this holy flame has been awakened lives in true happiness, content with everything and in everything free. He sees the cause of human corruption and knows that it is inevitable. He hates no criminal, he pities him, and seeks to raise him who has fallen, and to restore the wanderer, because he feels notwithstanding all the corruption, in the *whole* there is no taint.

He sees with a clear eye the underlying truth in the foundation of all religion, he knows the sources of superstition and of incredulity, as being caused by *modifications* of truth which have not attained perfect equilibrium.

We are assured, my esteemed brothers, that you consider the true Mystic from this aspect, and that you will not attribute to *his royal art*, that which the misdirected energy of some isolated individuals have made of this art.

It is, therefore, with these views, which accord exactly with ours, that you will compare religion, and the mysteries of the holy schools of Wisdom, to loving sisters who have watched over the good of mankind since the necessity of their birth.

Religion divides itself into exterior and interior religion, exterior signifying ceremony; and interior, worship in spirit and in truth; the outer schools possessing the letter and the symbol, the inner ones, the spirit and meaning—but the outer schools were united to the inner ones by ceremonies, as also the outer schools of the mysteries were linked with the inner one by means of symbol.

Thus religion can never be *merely* ceremony, but hidden and holy mysteries penetrate through symbol into the outer worship to prepare men properly for the worship of God in spirit and in truth.

Very soon the night of symbol will disappear, the light will bring forth the day and the mysteries no longer veiled will show themselves in the splendour of full truth.

The vestibule of nature, the temple of reason and the sanctuary of Revelation, will form but one Temple. Thus the great edifice will be completed, the edifice which consists in the re-union of man, nature, and God.

A perfect knowledge of man, of nature, and of God will be the lights which will enable the leaders of humanity to bring back from every side their wandering brothers, those who are led by the prejudices of reason, by the turbulence of passions, to the ways of peace and knowledge.

We are approaching the period of light, and the reign of wisdom and love, that of God who is the source of light; Brothers of light, there is but one religion whose simple truth spreads in all religions like branches, returning through multiplicity into the unity of the tree.

Sons of truth, there is but one order, but one Brotherhood, but one association of men thinking alike in the one object of acquiring the light. From this centre misunderstanding has caused innumerable Orders, but all will return from the multiplicity of opinions, to the only truth and to the true Order, the association of those who are able to receive the light, the *Community of the Elect.*

With this measure all religions and all orders of man must be measured. Multiplicity is in the ceremony of the exterior; truth only in the interior. The trend of these brotherhoods is in the variety of explanation of the symbols caused by the lapse of time, needs of the day, and other circumstances. The true Community of Light *can* be only one.

The exterior symbol is only the sheath which holds the inner; it may change and multiply, but it can never weaken the truth of the interior; moreover, it was necessary; we ought to seek it and try to decipher it to discover the meaning of the spiritual interior.

All errors, divisions, all mis-understandings in Religion and in secret societies only concern the letter. What rests behind it remains always pure and holy.

Soon the time for those who seek the light will be accomplished, for the day comes when the old will be united to the new, the outer to the inner, the high with the low, the heart with the brain, man with God, and this epoch is destined for the present age. Do not ask, beloved brothers, . . . why the present age? . . .

Everything has its time for beings subject to time and space. It is in such wise according to the unvarying law of the Wisdom of God, who has co-ordinated all in harmony and perfection.

The elect should first labour to acquire both wisdom and love, in order to earn the gift of power, which unchangeable Divinity gives only to those who *know* and those who *love.*

Morning follows night, and the sun rises, and all moves on to full mid-day, where all shadows disappear in his vertical splendour. Thus, the letter of truth must exist; then comes the practical explanation, then the truth itself; *only truth can comprehend truth*; then alone can the spirit of truth appear which sets the seals closing the light. He who now can receive the truth will understand. It is to you, much loved brothers, you who labour to reach truth, you who have so faithfully preserved the glyph of the holy mysteries in your temple, it is to you that the first ray of truth will be directed; this ray will pierce through the cloud of mystery, and will announce the full day and the treasure which it brings.

Do not ask *who* those are who write to you; look at the spirit not the letter, the thing, not at persons.

Neither pride, nor self seeking, neither does any unworthy motive, exist in our retreats; we know the object and the destination of man, and the light which lights us works in all our actions.

We are especially called to write to you, dear brothers of light; and that which gives power to our commission is the truth which we possess, and which we pass on to you on the least sign, and according to the measure of the capacity of each.

Light is apt for communication, where there is reception and capacity, but it constrains no one, and waits its reception tranquilly.

Our desire, our aim, our office is to revivify the dead letter, and to spiritualise the symbols, turn the passive into the active, death into life; but this we cannot do *by ourselves*, but through the spirit of light of Him who is Wisdom and the Light of the world.

Until the present time the Inner Sanctuary has been separated from the Temple, and the Temple beset with those who belong only to the precincts; but the time is coming when the Innermost will be re-united with the Temple, in order that those who are in the Temple can influence those who are in the outer courts, so that the outer pass in.

In our sanctuary all the hidden mysteries are preserved intact, they have never been profaned.

This sanctuary is invisible, as is a force which is only known through its action.

By this short description, my dear brothers, you can tell who we are, and it will be superfluous to assure you that we do not belong to those restless natures who seek to build in this common life an ideal after their own fantastic imaginations. Neither do we belong to those who wish to play a great part in the world, and who promise miracles that they themselves do not understand. We do not represent either that class of minds, who, resenting the condition of certain things, have no object but the desire of dominating others, and who love adventure and exaggeration.

We can also assure you that we belong to no other sect or association than the one true and great one of those who are able to receive the light. We are not also of those who think it their right to mould all after their own model, the arrogance to seek to re-model all other societies; we assure you faithfully that we know *exactly* the innermost of religion and of the Holy Mysteries; and that we possess with absolute certainty, all that has been surmised to be in the Adytum, and that this said possession gives us the strength to justify our commission, and to impart to the dead letter and hieroglyphic everywhere both spirit and life. The treasures in our sanctuary are many; we understand the spirit and meaning of all symbols and all ceremony which have existed since the day of Creation to the present time, as well as the most interior truths of all the Holy Books, with the laws and customs of primitive people.

We possess a light by which we are anointed, and

by means of which we read the hidden and secret things of nature.

We possess a fire which feeds us, and which gives us the strength to act upon everything in nature. We possess *a key to open* the gate of mystery, and *a key to shut* nature's laboratory. We know of the existence of a bond which will unite us to the Upper Worlds, and reveal to us their sights and their sounds. All the marvels of nature are subordinate to our will by *its* being united with Divinity.

We have mastered the science which draws directly from nature, whence there is no error, but truth and light only.

In our School we are instructed in all things because our Master is the Light itself and its essence. The plenitude of our scholarship is the knowledge of this tie between the divine and spiritual worlds and of the spiritual world with the elementary, and of the elementary world with the material world.

By these knowledges we are in condition to co-ordinate the spirits of nature and the heart of man.

Our science is the inheritance promised to the Elect; otherwise, those who are duly prepared for receiving the light, and the practice of our science is in the completion of the Divine union with the child of man.

We could often tell you, beloved brothers, of

marvels relating to the hidden things in the treasury of the Sanctuary, which would amaze and astonish you; we could speak to you about ideas concerning which the profoundest philosophy is as removed as the earth from the sun, but to which we are near being one with the light of the innermost.

But our object is not to excite your curiosity, but to raise your desires to seek the light at its source, where your search for wisdom will be rewarded and your longing for love satisfied, for wisdom and love dwell in our retreats. The stimulus of their reality and of their truth is our magical power.

We assure you that our treasures, though of infinite value, are concealed in so simple a manner that they entirely baffle the researches of opinionated science, and also though these treasures would bring to carnal minds both madness and sorrow, nevertheless, they are, and they ever remain to us the treasures of the highest wisdom.

My best blessing upon you, O my brothers, if you understand these great truths. The recovery of *the triple word* and of its power will be your reward.

Your happiness will be in having the strength to help to re-unite man with man, and with nature and with God, which is the real work of every workman who has not *rejected the Corner Stone.*

Now we have fulfilled our trust and we have announced the approach of full day, and the joining of the inner Sanctuary with the Temple; we leave the rest to your own free will.

We know well, to our bitter grief, that even as the Saviour was not understood in his personality, but was ridiculed and condemned in his humility, likewise also His spirit which will appear in glory will also be rejected and despised by many. Nevertheless the coming of His Spirit should be announced in the Temples in order that these words should be fulfilled.

"I have knocked at your doors and you have not opened them to me; I have called and you have not listened to my voice; I have invited you to the wedding, but you were busy with other things."

May Peace and the light of the Spirit be with you!

LETTER IV

As infinity in numbers loses itself in the unit, and as the innumerable rays of a circle are united in one single centre only, it is likewise with the Mysteries; their hieroglyphics and infinite number of emblems have the object of exemplifying but one single truth. He who knows this has found the key to understand everything all at once.

There is but one God, but one truth, and one way which leads to this grand Truth. There is but one means of finding it.

He who has found this way possesses everything in its possession: all wisdom in one book alone, all strength in one force, every beauty in one single object, all riches in one treasure only, every happiness in one perfect felicity. And the sum of all these perfections is Jesus Christ, who was crucified and who lived again. Now, this great truth, expressed thus, is, it is true, only an object of faith, but it can become also one of *experimental knowledge*, as soon as we are instructed *how* Jesus Christ can be or become all this.

This great mystery was always an object of instruction *in the Secret School of the invisible and interior Church;* this great knowledge was understood in the earliest days of Christianity under the name of *Disciplina Arcana*. From this secret school are derived all the rites and ceremonies extant in the Outer Church. But the spirit of these grand and simple verities was withdrawn into the Interior, and in our day it is entirely lost as to the exterior.

It has been prophesied long ago, dear brothers, that all which is hidden shall be revealed in these latter days; but it has also been predicted that many false prophets will arise, and the faithful are warned not to believe every spirit, but to prove them if they really come from God, 1 John iv. 5. The apostle himself explains how this truth is ascertained. He says, "Hereby know ye the Spirit of God, every spirit which confesseth that Jesus Christ is come in the flesh is of God, and every spirit which confesseth not is not of God." That is to say, the spirit who separates in Him the Divine and human *is not from God*.

We confess that Jesus Christ is come in the flesh, and hence the spirit of truth speaks by us. But the mystery that Jesus Christ is come *in the flesh* is of wide extent and great depth, and in it is contained the knowledge of the divine-human, and it is this knowledge that we are choosing to-day as object for our instruction.

As we are not speaking to neophytes in matters of faith, it will be much easier for you, dear brothers, to receive the sublime truths which we will present to you, as without doubt you have already chosen as object for your holy meditation various preparatory subjects.

Religion considered scientifically is the doctrine of the re-union of man separated from God to man re-united to God. Hence its sole object is to unite every human being to God, through which union alone can humanity attain its highest felicity both temporally and spiritually.

This doctrine, therefore, of *re-union* is of the most sublime importance, and being a doctrine it necessarily must have a method by which it leads and teaches us. The first is the knowledge of the correct means of re-union, and secondly the teaching, after the knowledge of the correct means, how these means should be suitably co-ordinated to the end.

This grand concept of re-union, on which all religious doctrine is concentrated, could never have been known to man *without* revelation. It has always been altogether outside the sphere of scientific knowledge, but this very ignoranuce of man has made revelation absolutely necessary to us, otherwise we could, unassisted, never have found the means of rising out of this state of ignorance.

Revelation entails the necessity of faith in revelation, because he who has no experience or knowledge whatsoever of a thing must necessarily believe that he wishes to know and have experience. If faith fails, there is no desire for revelation, and the mind of man closes by itself, its own door and road for discovering the methods revealed by Revelation only. As action and re-action follow each other in nature, so also inevitably revelation and faith act and re-act. One cannot exist without the other, and the more faith a man has the more will revelation be made to him of matters which lie in obscurity. It is true, and very true, that all the veiled truths of religions, even those heavily veiled ones, the most difficult ones to us, will one day be revealed and justified before a tribunal of the most rigid Justice; but the weakness of men, the lack of penetration in perceiving the relation and correspondence between physical and spiritual nature, requires that the highest truths should only be imparted gradually. The holy obscurity of the mysteries is thus on account of *our* weakness, because our eyes are enabled only gradually to bear their full and dazzling light. In every grade at which the believer in Revelation arrives, he obtains clearer light, and this progressive illumination continues the more convincing, because every truth of faith so acquired becomes more and more vitalised, passing finally into conviction.

Hence faith is founded on our weakness, and also on the full light of revelation which will, in its communication with us, direct us according to our capabilities to the gradual understanding of things, so that in due order the cognisance of the most elevated truths will be ours.

Those objects which are quite unknown to human sense are necessarily belonging to the domain of faith.

Man can only adore and be silent, but if he wishes to demonstrate matters which cannot be manifested objectively, he necessarily falls into error.

Man should adore and be silent, therefore, until such time arrives when these objects in the domain of faith become clearer, and, therefore, more easily recognised. Everything proves itself by itself as soon as we have acquired the interior *experience* of the truths revealed through faith, so soon as we are led by faith to vision, that is to say, to full cognisance.

In all time have there been men illuminated of God who had this interior knowledge of the things of faith demonstrated objectively either in full or partly, according as the truths of faith passed into their understanding or their hearts. The first kind of vision was called *divine illumination.* The second was entitled *divine inspiration.*

The inner sensorium was opened in many to divine and transcendental vision, called ecstacy because this inner sensorium was so enlarged that it entirely dominated the outer physical senses.

But this kind of man is always inexplicable, and he must remain such always to the man of mere sense who has no organs receptive to the transcendental and supernatural, "the natural man receiveth not the things of the Spirit of God, for they are foolishness unto him and he cannot know them, because they are spiritually judged," 1 Cor. xi. 14, *i.e.*, because his spiritual senses are not open to the transcendental world, so that he can have no more objective cognisance of such world than a blind man has of colour; thus the natural man has lost these interior senses, or rather, the capacity for their development is neglected almost to atrophy.

Thus mere physical man is, in general, spiritually blind, one of the further consequences of the Fall. Man then is doubly miserable; he not only has his eyes blindfolded to the sight of high truths, but his heart also languishes a prisoner in the bonds of flesh and blood, which confine him to animal and sensuous pleasures to the hurt of more elevated and genuine ones. Therefore, are we slaves to concupiscence, to the domination of tyrannical passions, and, therefore, do we drag ourselves as paralysed sufferers supported on crutches; the one crutch being the weak one of mere human reason, and the other, sentiment—the one daily giving us appearance instead of reality, the other making us constantly choose evil, imagining it to be good. This is, therefore, our unhappy condition.

Men can only be happy when the bandage which intercepts the true light falls from their eyes, and when the fetters of slavery are loosened from their hearts. The blind must see, the lame must walk, before happiness can be understood. But the great and all-powerful law to which the felicity or happiness of man is indissolubly attached is the one following—"Man, let reason rule over your passions!"

For ages has man striven to teach and to preach, with, however, the result, after so many centuries, of but the blind always leading the blind; for in all the foolishness of misery into which we have fallen, we do not yet see that man wants more than man to raise us from this condition.

Prejudices and errors, crimes and vices, only change from century to century; they are never extirpated from humanity; reason without illumination flickers faintly in every age, in the heavy air of spiritual darkness; the heart, exhausted with passions, is also the same century after century.

There is but One who can heal these evils, but One who is able to open our inner eyes, but One who can free us from the bonds of sensuality.

This One is Jesus Christ, the *Saviour of Man*, the *Saviour* because He wishes to obliterate from us all the consequences which follow as result from the blindness of our natural reason, or the errors arising from the passions of ungoverned hearts.

Very few men, beloved brothers, have a true and exact conception of the *greatness* of the idea meant by the Redemption of Man; many suppose that Jesus Christ the Lord has only redeemed or rebought us by His Blood from *damnation, otherwise the eternal separation* of man from God; but they do not believe that He could also deliver all those who are bound in Him and confide in Him, from all the miseries of this earth plane!

Jesus Christ is the Saviour of the World; He is the deliverer from all human wretchedness, and He has redeemed us from death and sin; how could He be all that, if the world must languish perpetually in the shades of ignorance and in the bonds of passions? It has been already very clearly predicted in the Prophets that the time of the Redemption of His people, the first Sabbath of time, *will come*. Long ago ought we to have acknowledged this most consolatory promise; but the *want* of the true knowledge of God, of man, and of nature has been the real hindrance which has always obstructed our sight of the great Mysteries of the faith.

You must know, my brothers, that there is a dual nature, one pure, spiritual, immortal, and indestructible, the other impure, material, mortal, and destructible. The pure nature was before the impure. This latter originated solely through the disharmony and disproportion of substances which form destructible nature. Hence nothing is permanent until all disproportions and dissonances are eradicated, so that all remains in harmony.

The incorrect conception regarding spirit and matter is one of the principal causes which prevent many verities of faith from shining in their true lustre.

Spirit is a substance, an essence, an absolute reality. Hence its properties are indestructibility, uniformity, penetration, indivisibility, and continuity. Matter is not a substance, it is *an aggregate.* Hence it is destructible, divisible, and subject to change.

The metaphysical world is one *really existing* perfectly pure and indestructible, whose Centre we call Jesus Christ, and whose inhabitants are known by the names of Angels and Spirits.

The physical world is that of phenomena, and it possesses no absolute truth, all that we call truth here is but relative, the shadow and phenomena only of truth.

Our reason here borrows all its ideas from the senses, hence they are lifeless and dead. We draw everything from external objectivity, and our reason is like an ape who imitates what nature shows him outwardly. Thus the light of the senses is the principle of our earthly reason, sensuality the motive for our will, tending therefore to animal wants and their satisfaction. It is true, however, that we feel higher motives imperative, but up to the present we do not know either where to seek or where to find.

In this world everything is corruptible; it is useless to seek here for a pure *principle* of reason and morality or motive for the Will. This must be sought for in a more exalted world—there, where all is pure and indestructible, where there reigns a Being all wisdom and all love. Thus the world neither can nor will become happy until this Real Being can be received by humanity in full and become its All in All.

Man, dear brothers, is composed of indestructible and metaphysical substance, as well as of material and destructible substance, but in such a manner that the indestructible and eternal is, as it were, *imprisoned* in the destructible matter.

Thus two contradictory natures are comprehended in the same man. The destructible substance enchains us to the sensible, the other seeks to deliver us from these chains, and to raise us to the spiritual. Hence the incessant combat between good and evil.

The fundamental cause of human corruption is to be found in the corruptible matter from which man is formed. For this gross matter oppresses the action of the transcendental and spiritual principle, and is the true cause, hence, of the blindness of our understanding, and the errors of our inclinations.

The fragility of a china vessel depends upon the clay from which it is formed. The most beautiful form that clay of any sort is able to receive must always remain fragile because the matter of which it is formed is also fragile. Thus do men remain likewise frail notwithstanding all our external culture.

When we examine the causes of the obstacles

keeping the natural man in such deep abasement, they are found in the grossness of the matter in which the spiritual part is, as it were, buried and bound.

The inflexibility of fibres, the immovability of temperaments, that would wish to obey the refined stimulation of the spirit, are, as it were, the material chains which bind them, preventing in us the action of the sublime functions of which the spirit is capable.

The nerves and fluidity of the brain can only yield us rough and obscure notions derived from phenomena, and not from truth and the things themselves; and as we cannot, by the strength of our thinking powers alone, have sufficient balance to oppose representations strong enough to counteract the violence of external sensation, the result is that we are governed by our sensations, and the voice of reason which speaks softly internally is deafened by the tumultuous noise of the elements which keep our mechanism going.

It is true that reason strains to raise itself above this uproar, and wishes to decide the combat, seeking to restore order by the light and force of its judgment. But its action is only like the rays of the sun constantly hidden by clouds.

The grossness of all the matter in which material man consists, and the tissue of the whole edifice of his nature, is the cause of that disinclination which holds the soul in continual imperfection.

The heaviness of our thinking power in general is consequent upon dependence upon gross and unyielding matter, this same matter forming the true bonds of the flesh, and is the true source of all error and vice. Reason, which should be an absolute legislator, is continually slave to sensuality, which raises itself as regent and, governing the reason that is drooping in chains, follows its own desires.

This truth has been felt for long, and it has always been taught that reason should be sole legislator. It should govern the will and never be governed itself.

Great and small feel this truth; but no sooner is it desired to put it in execution than the animal will vanquishes reason, and then the reason subjugates the animal will; thus in every man the victory and defeat are alternate, hence this power and counter-power are the cause of this perpetual oscillation between good and evil, or the true and the false.

If man wishes to be led to the true in such manner that we can only act after the laws of reason, and from the purified will, it is absolutely necessary to constitute the pure reason sovereign in man. But how can this be done when the matter out of which many men is formed is more or less brutal, divisible and corruptible, hence misery, illness, poverty, death, want, prejudices, errors, and vices, the necessary consequence of the limitation of the immortal spirit in the bonds of brute and corruptible matter. Sensuality is bound to rule if reason be fettered.

Yes, friends and brothers, such is the general fate of man, and as this state of things is propagated from man to man, it may in all justice be called the hereditary corruption of man.

We observe, in general, that the powers of reason act upon the heart, but in relation only to the specific constitution of the matter of which man is made. Thus it is extremely remarkable when we think that the sun vivifies this animal matter according to the measure of the distance from this terrestrial body, that it makes it suitable to the functions of animal economy, but at one degree more or less raised from spiritual influence. Diversity of nations, their properties with regard to climate, the variety of character, passions, manners, prejudices and customs, even their virtues and their vices, depend entirely upon the specific constitution of the matter from which they are formed, and in which the imprisoned spirit operates accordingly. Man's capacity for culture is modified to this constitution, likewise his science, which can only affect people as far as there is matter present, susceptible to such modification, and in this modification consists the capacity for culture suitable to such people, which suitability depends partly on climate, partly on descent.

Generally, we find in each zone man much the

same everywhere, weak and sensual, wise just in so far as his physical matter allows reason to triumph over the sensuous, or foolish if the sensuous obtains mastery over the more or less fettered spirit. In this lies the evil and the good specially belonging to each nation, as well as to each isolated individual. We find in the world at large the same corruption inherent in the matter from which man is made, only under various forms and modifications.

From the lowest animal condition of savage nature man rises to the idea of the social state, primarily through his wants and desires, strength and cunning, qualities especially animal, inherently his *as* the animal develops thence gradually into other forms.

The modifications of these fundamental animal tendencies are endless; and the highest degree to which human culture as acquired by the world, has attained, up to the present has not carried things further than the putting of a finer polish on the substance of his animal instincts. This means to say we are raised from the rank of the brute to that of the refined animal.

But this period was necessary, because on its accomplishment begins a new era, when the animal instincts being fully developed, there commences the stage of evolution of the more elevated desires towards light and reason.

Jesus Christ has written in our hearts in exceedingly beautiful words this great truth, that man must seek in his common clay for the cause of all his sorrows. When He said, "The best man, he who strives the most to arrive at truth, sins seven times a day," He wished to say by this, in the man of the finest organisation, the seven powers of the spirit are still closed, therefore the seven sensuous actions surmount them daily after their respective fashions.

Thus the best man is exposed to error and passions; the best man is weak and sinful; the best man is not a free man, and, therefore, exempt from pain and trouble; the best man is subject to sickness and death, and why? Because all these are the natural inevitable consequences incidental to the qualities of the corrupt matter of which he is formed.

Therefore, there could be no hope of higher happiness for humanity so long as this corruptible and material forms the principal substantial part of his being.

The impossibility of mankind to transport itself, of itself, to true perfection, is a despairing thought, but, at the same time, one full of consolation, because, in consequence of this radical impossibility, and because of it, a more exalted and perfect being than man permitted himself to be clothed in this mortal and destructible envelope *in order* to make the mortal immortal, and the destructible indestructible; and in this object is to be sought the true reason for the Incarnation of Jesus Christ.

Jesus Christ, the Son of God, the actual substantial Word by which all is made, and which existed from the beginning, Jesus Christ, the Wisdom of God working in everything, was as the centre of Paradise of the world and of light. He was the only real organism by which alone Divine strength could be communicated, and this organism is of immortal and pure nature, that indestructible substance which gives new life and raises all things to happiness and perfection. This pure incorruptible substance is *the pure element* in which spiritual man lived.

From this perfect element, which God only can inhabit, and the substance out of which the first man was formed, from it was the first man separated by the Fall. By the partaking of the Tree of Good and Evil, of the mixture, the good and incorruptible principle with the bad and corruptible one, he was self-poisoned, so that his immortal essence retreated interiorly, and the mortal, pressing forward, clothed him externally. Thus, then, disappeared immortality, happiness, and life, and mortality and death were the results of this change.

Many men cannot understand the idea of the Tree of Good and Evil; this tree was, however, the product of moveable but central matter, but in which destructibility had somewhat the superiority over the indestructible. The premature use of this fruit was that which poisoned Adam, robbing him of his immortality and enveloping him in this material and mortal clay, and thenceforward he fell a prey to the Elements *which originally he governed.* This unhappy event was, however, the reason why Immortal Wisdom, the pure metaphysical element, clothed itself with a mortal body and voluntarily sacrificed himself, so that the Interior Powers could penetrate into the centre of the destruction, and could then ferment gradually, changing the mortal to the immortal.

Thus, when it came about quite naturally that immortal man became subject to mortality through the enjoyment of mortal matter, it also happened quite naturally that mortal man could only recover his former dignity through the enjoyment of Immortal Matter.

All passes naturally and simply under God's Reign, but in order to understand this simplicity it is requisite to have pure ideas of God, of nature, and of man. And if the sublimest Truths of faith are still, for us, wrapped in impenetrable obscurity, the reason for this is because we have up to the present dissolved the connection between God, nature, and man.

Jesus Christ has spoken to His most intimate friends when He was still on this earth, of the grand mystery of Regeneration, but all that He said was obscure to them, they could not then receive it; thus the development of these great

Truths was reserved for latter days, for it is the greatest and the last Mystery of Religion, in which all the others retreat as to a Unity.

Regeneration is no other than a dissolution of, and a release from this impure and corruptible matter, which enchains our immortal essence, plunging into deathly sleep its obstructed vital force. Therefore, there must necessarily be a real method to eradicate this poisonous ferment which breeds so much suffering for us, and thereby to liberate the obstructed vitality.

There is, however, no other means to find this excepting by religion, for religion looked at scientifically being the doctrine which proclaims the re-union with God, it must of necessity show us how to arrive at this re-union.

Is not Jesus the life giving intelligence? He gives us the principal object of the Bible and of all the desires, hopes, and efforts of the Christians. Have we not received from our Lord and Master while still He walked with His disciples, the profoundest solutions of the most hidden truths? Did not our Lord and Master when He was with them in His glorfied Body after His resurrection give them the highest revelation with regard to His Person, and did He not lead them still more deeply into central knowledge of truth?

Will He not realise that which He said in His Sacerdotal prayer, St. John xvii. 22, 23: "And the glory which thou hast given to me I have given unto them, that they may be one, even as We are one: I in them, and they in Me, that they may be perfected into One."

As the disciples of the Lord could not comprehend this great mystery of the new and last alliance, Jesus Christ transmitted it to the latter days, of the future now arriving, when He said, "And the glory which Thou hast given Me, I have given unto them, that they may be one even as We are One," St. John xvii. 22. This alliance is called the Union of Peace. It is then that the law of God will be engraven in the heart of our hearts; we shall all know the Lord; and we shall be His people, and He will be our God.

All is already prepared for this actual possession of God, this union with God really possible here below; and the holy element, the efficacious medicine for humanity, is revealed by God's Spirit. The table of the Lord is ready and everyone is invited; the "true bread of Angels" is prepared.

The holiness and the greatness of the Mystery which contains within itself every mystery here obliges us to be silent, and we are not permitted to speak more than concerning its effects.

The corruptible and destructible is destroyed, and replaced by the incorruptible and by the indestructible. The inner sensorium opens and links us on to the spiritual world. We are enlightened by wisdom, led by truth, and nourished with the torch of love. Unimagined strength develops in us wherewith to vanquish the world, the flesh and the devil. Our whole being is renewed and made suitable for the actual dwelling-place of the Spirit of God. Command over nature, intercourse with the upper worlds, and the delight of visible intercourse with the Lord are granted also!

The hoodwink of ignorance falls from our eyes, the bonds of sensuality break, and we rejoice in the liberty of God's children.

We have told you the chiefest and most important fact, if your heart having the thirst for truth has laid hold on the pure ideas that you have gathered from all this, and have received in its entirety the grandeur and the blessedness of the thing itself as object of desire, we will tell you further.

May the Glory of the Lord and the renewing of your whole being be meanwhile the highest of your hopes!

LETTER V

IN our last letter, my dear brothers (and sisters), you granted me your earnest attention to that highest of mysteries, *the real possession of God;* it is therefore necessary to give you fuller light on this subject.

Man, as we know, is unhappy in this world because he is made out of destructible matter that is subject to trouble and sorrow.

The fragile envelope—*i.e.*, his body—exposes him to the violence of the elements, pain, poverty, suffering, illnesses. This is his normal fate; his immortal spirit languishing in the bonds of sense. Man is unhappy, because he is ill in body and soul, and he possesses no true panacea either for his body or for his soul.

Those whose duty it is to govern and lead other men to happiness, are as other men, also weak and subject to the same passions and prejudices.

Therefore, what fate can humanity expect? Must the greater part of it be always unfortunate? Is there no salvation for all?

Brothers, if humanity as a whole is ever capable of being raised to a condition of true happiness, such state can only be possible under the following conditions:—

First, poverty, pain, illness and sorrow must become much less frequent. Secondly, passions, prejudices and ignorance must diminish.

Is this at all possible with the nature of man, when experience proves that, from century to century, suffering only assumes fresh form; that passions, prejudices and errors always cause the same evils; and when we realise that all these things only change shape, and that man in every age remains much the same weak man?

There is a terrible judgment pronounced upon the human race, and this judgment is—men can never become happy so long as they will not become wise; but they will never become wise, while sensuality governs reason, while the spirit languishes in the bonds of flesh and blood.

Where is the man that has no passions? Let him shew himself. Do we not all wear the chains of sensuality more or less heavily? Are we not all slaves? All sinners?

This realisation of our low estate excites in us the desire to be raised beyond it, and we lift up our eyes on high, and an angel's voice says—*the sorrows of man shall be comforted.*

Man being sick body and soul, this mortal sickness must have a cause, and *this cause* is to be found in the very matter out of which man is made.

The destructible imprisons the indestructible, the *ferment of sin* is in us, and in this ferment is human corruption, and its propagation and consequences form the perpetuation of original sin.

The healing of humanity is only possible through the destruction of this ferment of sin, hence we have need of a physician and a remedy that really can cure us. But an invalid cannot be cured by another; the man of destructible matter cannot re-make himself of indestructible matter; dead matter cannot awake other dead, the blind cannot lead the blind.

Only the Perfect can bring anything to perfection; only the Indestructible can make the destructible likewise; only the Living can wake the dead.

This Physician and this active Medicine cannot be found in death and destruction, only in superior nature where all is perfection and life!

The lack of the knowledge of the union of Divinity with nature, nature with man, is the true cause of all prejudice and error. Theologians, philosophers, moralists, all wish to regulate the world, and they fill it with endless contradictions.

Theologians do not see the union of God with nature and fall therefore into error.

Modern philosophers study only matter, and not the connection of pure nature with divine nature, and therefore announce the falsest opinions.

Moralists will not recognise the inherent corruption of human nature, and they expect to cure by words, when means are absolutely necessary.

Thus the world, man and God, continue in permanent dissension ; one opinion drives out another ; superstition and incredulity take turn about in dominating society, separating man from the word of truth when he has so much dire need of approaching her.

It is only in the true Schools of Wisdom that one can learn to know God, nature, and man ; and in these, for thousands of years, has work been done in silence to acquire to the highest degree this knowledge,—the union of man with pure nature and with God.

This great object, God and Nature, to which everything tends, has been represented to man symbolically in every religion ; and all the symbols and holy glyphs are but the letter by which man can gradually, step by step, recover the highest of all divine mysteries, natural and human, and learn the means of healing his unhappy condition, and of the union of his being with pure nature and with God.

We have attained this epoch solely under God's guidance. Divinity, next remembering its covenant with man, has given forth the means of cure for suffering mankind, and shewn thereby how to raise man to his original dignity, uniting him to God, the Source of his happiness.

The knowledge of this method ensuring recovery

is the science of Saints and of the Elect, and its possession the inheritance promised to God's children.

Now, my beloved brothers, I want you to grant me your most earnest attention to what I am about to say.

In our blood there is lying concealed a slimy matter (called the gluten) which has a nearer kinship to animal than to spiritual man. This gluten is the body of sin.

This material, this matter, can be modified in various manners, according to the stimulus of sense; and according to the kind of modification and change occurring in this body or matter of sin, so also vary the diverse sinful tendencies of man.

In its most violent expansion this matter produces pride; in its utmost contraction, avarice, self-will and selfishness; in its repulsion, rage and anger; in its circular movements levity and incontinence; in its eccentricity, greediness and drunkenness; in its concentricity, envy; in its essence, sloth.

This ferment of sin, as original sin, is more or less working in the blood of every man, and is transmitted from father to son, and the perpetual propagation of this baneful material, everlastingly hinders the simultaneous action of spirit with matter.

It is quite true that man by his will-power can put limits to the action of this body of sin, and can dominate it so that it becomes less active, but to destroy and annihilate it altogether is beyond his power. This then is the cause of the combat we are constantly waging between the good and the evil in us.

This body of sin which is in us, forms the ties of flesh and blood which, on the one side, bind us to our immortal spirit, and, on the other, to the tendencies of the animal man. It is as it were the allurements of the animal passions that smoulder and take fire at last.

The violent reaction of this body of sin in us, on sensuous stimulation, is the reason why we choose, for the want of calm and tranquil judgment, rather the evil than the good, because the active fermentation of this matter impedes the quiet action of the spirit necessary to instruct and sustain the reason.

This same evil matter is also the cause of our ignorance, because, as its thick and inflexible substance surcharges the fine brain fibres, it prevents the co-action of reason, which is required to penetrate the objects of the understanding.

Thus falseness and all evils are the properties of this sinful matter, this body of sin, just as the good and the true are the essential qualities of the spiritual principle within us.

Through the recognition and thorough understanding by us of this body of sin we learn to see that we are beings morally ill, that we have need of a physician who can give us a medicine which will destroy and eradicate the evil matter always fermenting banefully within us, a remedy that will cure us and restore us to moral health.

We learn also clearly to recognize that all mere moralizing with words is of little use *when real means are necessary.*

We have been moralizing in varied words for centuries, but the world remains pretty much the same. A doctor would do but little good in talking only of his remedies, it is necessary for him actually to prescribe his medicines; he has, however, first to see the real state of the sick person.

The condition of humanity—the moral sickness of man—is a true case of poisoning, consequent upon the eating of the fruit of the tree in which corruptible matter had the superiority.

The first effect of this poison resulted thus: the incorruptible principle, the body of life as opposed to the body of sin or death, whose expansion caused the perfection of Adam, concentrated itself inwardly, and the external part was abandoned to the government of the elements. Hence a mortal matter gradually covered the immortal essence, and the loss of this central light was the cause subsequently of all man's sufferings.

Communication with the world of light was interrupted, the interior eye which had the power of seeing truth *objectively* was closed, and the physical eye opened to the plane of changing phenomena.

Man lost all true happiness, and in this unhappy condition he would have for ever lost all means of restoration to health were it not that the love and mercy of God, who had no other object in creation but the greatest happiness for its creatures, immediately afforded to fallen man a means of recovery. In this means, he, with all posterity, had the right to trust, in order that while still in his state of banishment, he might support his misfortune with humility and resignation, and, moreover, find in his pilgrimage the great consolation, that every corruptible thing in man could be restored perfectly through the love of a Saviour.

Despair would have been the fate of man without such revelation.

Man, before the Fall, was the living Temple of Divinity, and at the time when this Temple was destroyed, the plan to rebuild the Temple was already projected by the Wisdom of God; and at this period begin the Holy Mysteries of every religion, which are all and each in themselves, after a thousand varying modes, according to time and circumstances, and method of conception of different nations, but symbols repeated and modified of one solitary truth, and this unique truth is —*regeneration, or the re-union of man with God.*

Before the Fall man was wise, he was united to Wisdom; after the Fall he was no longer one with Her, hence a true science through express Revelation became absolutely necessary.

The Revelation was the following :—

The condition of immortality consists in immortality permeating the mortal. Immortal substance is divine substance, and is no other than the magnificence of the Almighty throughout nature, the substance of the world and spirits, the infinity, in short, of God in whom all things move and have their being.

It is an immutable law, no creature can be truly happy when separated from the source of all happiness. This source, this *in whom*, is the magnificence of God Himself.

Through the partaking of destructible nourishment, man himself became destructible and material; matter, therefore, as it were places itself between God and man, that is to say, man is not directly penetrated and permeated by divinity, and, in consequence, he is thenceforth subject to, and falls under the dominion of, the laws regulating matter.

The divine in man, imprisoned by the bonds of this matter, is his immortal part, the part that should be at liberty, in order that its development should once again rule the mortal. Then once more does man regain his original greatness.

But a means for his cure, and a method to externalize what is now hidden and concealed within, is requisite. Fallen and unwise man of himself can neither know nor grasp this expedient; he cannot even recognise it, because he has lost pure knowledge and the light of true wisdom; he cannot take hold of it, because this remedy is infolded in interior nature, and he has neither the strength or power to unlock this hidden force.

Hence Revelation to learn this means, and strength to acquire this power, are necessary to man.

This necessity for the salvation of man was the cause of the determination of Wisdom, or the Son of God, to give Himself to be known by man, *being the pure substance out of which* all has been made. In this pure substance all power is reserved to vivify all dead substance, and to purify all that is impure.

But before that could be done, and the inmost part of man, the divine in him, be once more penetrated and re-opened again, and the whole world be regenerated, it was requisite that this divine substance should incarnate in humanity and become human, and therein transmit the divine and regenerative force to humanity; it was necessary also that this divine human form should be killed, in order that the divine and incorruptible substance contained in the blood should penetrate into the recesses of the earth, and thenceforth work a gradual dissolution of corruptible matter, so that in due time a pure and regenerated earth will be presented to man, with the Tree of Life growing once more, so that by partaking of its fruit, containing the true immortal essence, mortality in us will be once more annihilated, and man healed by the fruit of the Tree of Life, just as he was once poisoned by the partaking of the fruit of death.

This fact is the first and most important revelation and it embraces all, and it has been carefully preserved from mouth to mouth among the Chosen of God up to this time.

Human nature required a Saviour, this Saviour was Jesus Christ, the Wisdom of God itself, reality from God. He put on the envelope of humanity, to communicate *directly* the divine and immortal substance once more to the world, which was nothing else *but Himself.*

He offered himself voluntarily, in order that the *pure essential force* in His blood could penetrate directly, bringing with it the potentiality of all perfection to the hidden recesses of the earth.

Himself, both as High Priest and as Victim at the same time, entered into the Holy of Holies, and after having accomplished all that was necessary, he laid the foundation of the Royal Priesthood of His Elect, and taught these through the knowledge of His person and of His powers; now they should lead, as the first born of the spirit, other men, their brethren, to universal happiness.

And here begin the Sacerdotal Mysteries of the Elect and of the Inner Church.

The Royal and Priestly Science is that of Regeneration. It is called *Royal Science* because it leads man to power and the dominion over Nature.

It is called Sacerdotal, because it sanctifies and

brings all to perfection, spreading blessing and goodness everywhere.

This Science owes its immediate origin to the *verbal revelation* of God, it is always the Science of the Inner Church of Prophets and of Saints, and it recognised no other High Priest but Jesus Christ the Lord.

This Science has a triple object; first, regenerating the individual and isolated man, or the first of the Elect; second, many men; thirdly, all humanity.

Its exercise consists in the highest perfecting of itself and of everything in Nature.

This Science was never taught otherwise than by the Holy Spirit of God, and by those who were in unison with this Spirit, and it is beyond all other sciences, because it can alone teach the knowledge of God, of nature, and of man in a perfect harmony; while other sciences do not understand truly either God or nature, neither man nor his destination.

The capabilities of this Science are the powers to know God in man, and divinity in nature; these being, as it were, the Divine impression or seals, by which our inner selves can be opened and can arrive at union with Divinity.

Thus the re-union was the most exalted aim, and hence the Priesthood derived its name *religio, clerus regenerans.*

Melchizedek was the first Priest King; all true Priests of God and of Nature descend from him, and Jesus Christ himself was united with him as "priest" after the order of Melchizedek. This word is literally of the highest and widest significance and extent—מלכיצ־דק (MLKIZ-DQ). It means literally the introducing of the true substance of vital life, and the separation of this true vital substance from the mortal envelope which encloses it.

A priest is one who separates that which is pure nature from that which is of impure nature, a separator of the substance which contains all from the destructible matter which occasions pain and misery. The sacrifice or that which has been separated consists in bread and wine.

Bread means literally the substance which contains all; wine the substance which vitalizes everything.

Therefore, a priest after the order of Melchizedek is one who knows how to separate the all-embracing and vitalizing substance from impure matter, one who knows how to employ it as a real means of reconciliation and of re-union for fallen humanity, in order to communicate to him his true and royal privilege of power over nature, and the Sacerdotal dignity or the ability to unite himself by grace to the upper worlds.

In these few words is contained all the mystery of God's Priesthood, and the occupation and aim of the Priest.

But this royal Priesthood was only able to reach perfect maturity when Jesus Christ Himself as High

Priest had fulfilled the greatest of all sacrifices, and had entered into the Holy Sanctuary.

Here we are now entering on new and great mysteries worthy, I entreat you, of your most earnest attention.

When, according to the wisdom and justice of God, it was resolved to save the fallen human race, the Wisdom of God had to choose the method which afforded in every aspect the most efficacious means for the consummation of this great object.

When man became so thoroughly poisoned by the fruit of evil, carrying in himself henceforth the ferment of death, all around him became subject to death and destruction, therefore, divine mercy was bound to establish a counter remedy, which could be partaken of, containing within itself the divine and revitalising substance, so that by taking this immortal food, poisoned and death-stricken man could be healed and rescued from his suffering. But in order that this Tree of Life could be re-planted, it was requisite beyond all things that the corruptible material in the centre of the earth should be first regenerated, resolved and made capable of being again one day a universally vitalising substance.

This capacity for new life, bringing about the dissolution of corruptible essence which is inherent in the centre of the earth, was, however, possible to no other matter than divine vital substance enveloped in flesh and blood which could transmit the hidden forces of life to dead nature. This was done through the death of Jesus Christ. *The tinctural force* which flowed from His shed blood penetrated to the innermost parts of the earth, raised the dead, rent the rocks, and caused the total eclipse of the sun when it pressed from the centre of the earth where the light penetrated the central darkness to the circumference, and there laid the foundation of the future glorification of the world.

Since the death of Jesus Christ, the divine force, driven to the earth's centre by the shedding of His blood, works and ferments perpetually to press outward, and to fit and prepare all substances gradually for the great cataclysm which is destined for the world.

But the rebuilding of the world's edifice in general was not only the aim of Redemption. Man was the principal object for the shedding of Christ's blood, and to procure for him already in this material world the highest possible perfection by the amelioration of his being, Jesus Christ submitted to infinite suffering.

He is the Saviour of the world and of man. The object and cause of His Incarnation was to rescue us from sin, misery, and from death.

Jesus Christ has delivered us from all evil by His flesh, which he sacrificed, and by His blood, which He shed for us.

In the clear understanding of what consists this *flesh* and this *blood* of Jesus Christ lies the true and pure knowledge of the real regeneration of man.

The mystery of being united with Jesus Christ, not only spiritually *but also corporeally*, is the greatest aim of the Inner Church. Become one with Him in spirit and in being is the fulfilling and plenitude of the efforts of the Elect.

The means for this real possession of God is hidden from the wise of this world, and revealed to the simplicity of children.

Vain philosopher, bend thyself before the grand and Divine Mysteries that thou in thy wisdom canst not understand, and for the penetration of whose secrets the feeble light of human reason darkened by sense can give thee no measure!

LETTER VI AND LAST

GOD made Himself man to deify man. Heaven united itself with earth to transform earth into Heaven.

But in order that these divine transformations can take place, an entire change, a complete and absolute overturning and upsetting of our being, is necessary.

This change, this upsetting, is called re-birth. *To be born*, simply means to enter into a world in which the senses dominate, in which wisdom and love languish in the bonds of individuality.

To be *re-born* means to return to a world where the spirit of wisdom and love governs, and where animal-man obeys.

The re-birth is triple; first, the re-birth of our intelligence; second, of our heart and of our will; and, finally, the re-birth of our entire being.

The first and second kinds are called the spiritual, and the third the corporeal re-birth.

Many pious men, seekers after God, have been regenerated in the mind and will, but few have known the corporeal re-birth. This last has been attained to but by few men, and those to whom it has been given have only received it that they might serve as *agents* of God, in accordance with great and grand objects and intentions, and to bring humanity nearer to felicity.

It is now necessary, my dear brothers, to lay before you the true order of re-birth. God, who is all strength, wisdom, and love, works eternally in order and in harmony.

He who will not receive the spiritual life, he who is not born anew from the Lord, can not enter into heaven.

Man is engendered through his parents in original sin, that is to say, he enters into the natural life and not the spiritual.

The spiritual life consists in loving God above everything, and your neighbour as yourself. In this double-love consists the *principle* of the new life.

Man is begotten in evil, in the love of himself and of the things of this world. Love of himself! Self interest! Self gratification! Such are the substantial properties of evil. The good is in the love of God and your neighbour, in knowing no other love but the love of mankind, no interest but that affecting every man, and no other pleasure but that of the well-being of all.

It is by such sentiments that the spirit of the children of God is distinguished from the spirit of the children of this world.

To change the spirit of this world into the spirit of the children of God is to be regenerated, and it means to despoil the old man, and to re-clothe the new.

But no person can be re-born if he does not know and put in practice the following principle—that of truth becoming the object for our doing or not doing; therefore, he who desires to be re-born ought first to know what belongs to re-birth. He ought to understand, meditate, and reflect on all this. Afterwards he should act according to his knowledge, and the result will be a new life.

Now, as it is first necessary to know, and to be instructed in all that appertains to re-birth, a doctor, or an instructor is required, and if we know one, faith in him is also necessary, because of what use is an instructor if his pupil have no faith in him?

Hence, the commencement of re-birth is faith in Revelation.

The disciple should begin by believing that the Lord, the Son, is the Wisdom of God, that He is from all Eternity from God, and that He came into the world to bring happiness to humanity. He should believe that the Lord has full power in heaven and on earth, and that all faith and love, all the true and the good, come from Him alone; that He is the Mediator, the Saviour, and Governor of men.

When this most exalting faith has taken root in us, we shall think often of the Saviour, and these thoughts turned towards Him develop, and by His grace reacting in us, the seven closed and spiritual powers are opened.

The way to happiness.—Do you wish, man and brother, to acquire the highest happiness possible? Search for truth, wisdom, and love. But you will not find truth, wisdom, and love, save in the unity of the Lord Jesus Christ, the Anointed of God.

Seek, then, Jesus Christ with all your strength, search Him from the fulness of your heart.

The beginning of His Ascension is the knowledge of His absence, and from the recognition of this knowledge is the desire for increased power to seek Him, which desire is the beginning of faith.

Faith gives confidence, but faith has also its order of progress. First comes historic faith, then moral, then divine, and finally *living* faith. The progression is as follows: Historical faith when we learn to believe the history of Jesus of Nazareth, and through this simple historical faith in the *existence* of Jesus, will evolve moral faith, whose development consists in the acquirement of virtue by its search and practice, so that we see and find real pleasure in all that is taught by this Man; we find that His simple doctrine is full of wisdom and His teaching full of love; that His intentions towards humanity are straight and true, and that He willingly suffered death for the sake of justice. Thus, faith in His Person will be followed by faith in His Divinity.

This same Jesus Christ tells us now that He

is Son of God, and He emphasizes His words by instructing His disciples in the sacred mysteries of nature and religion.

Here natural and reasonable faith changes into divine faith, and we begin to believe that he was God made man. From this faith it results that we hold as true all that we do not yet understand, but which He tells us to believe. Through this faith in the Divinity of Jesus, and by that entire surrender to Him, and the faithful attention to His directions, is at last produced that living faith, by which we find *within ourselves* and TRUE through *our own experience*, all that hitherto we have until now believed in merely with the confidence of a child; and this living faith proved by experience is the highest grade of all.

When our hearts, through living faith, have received Jesus Christ into them, then this Light of the World is born within us as in a humble stable.

Everything in us is impure, surrounded by the spider-webs of vanity, covered with the mud of sensuality.

Our will is the Ox that is under the yoke of its passions. Our reason is the Ass who is bound through the obstinacy of its opinions, its prejudices, its follies.

In this miserable and ruined hut, the home of all the animal passions, can Jesus Christ be born in us through faith.

The simplicity of our souls, is as the shepherds who brought their first offerings, until at last the three principal powers of our royal dignity, our reason, our will, and our activity * prostrate themselves before Him and offer Him the gifts of truth, wisdom, and love.

Little by little, the stable of our hearts changes itself into an exterior Temple, where Jesus Christ teaches, but this Temple is still full of Scribes and Pharisees.

Those who sell, Dives and the money changers, are still to be found, and these should be driven out, and the Temple changed into a House of Prayer.

Little by little Jesus Christ chooses all the good powers in us to announce Him. He heals our blindness, purifies our leprosy, raises the dead powers into living forces within us; He is crucified in us, He dies, and He is gloriously raised again Conqueror with us. Afterwards His personality lives in us, and instructs us in exalted mysteries, until He has made us complete and ready for the perfect Regeneration when He mounts to heaven and thence sends us the Spirit of Truth.

But before such a Spirit can act in us we experience the following changes:—

First, the seven powers of our understanding are lifted up within us; afterwards, the seven powers of our hearts or of our will, and this exaltation takes

* The Three Magi.

place after the following manner. The human understanding is divided into seven powers; the first is that of looking at abstract objects—*intuitus.* By the second we perceive the objects abstractedly regarded—*apperceptio.* By the third, that which has been perceived is reflected upon—*reflexio.* The fourth is that of considering these objects in their diversity—*fantasia, imaginatio.* The fifth is that of deciding upon some thing—*judicium.* The sixth co-ordinates all these according to their relationships—*ratio.* The seventh and last is the power of realizing the whole intellectual intuition—*intellectus.*

This last contains, so to say, the sum of all the others.

The will of man divides itself similarly into seven powers, which, taken together as a unit, form the will of man, being, as it were, its *substantial* parts.

The first is the capacity of desiring things apart from himself—*desiderium.* The second is the power to annex mentally things desired for himself—*appetitus.* The third is the power of giving them form, realizing them so as to satisfy his desire—*concupiscentia.* The fourth is that of receiving inclinations, without deciding upon acting upon any, as in the condition of passion—*passio.* The fifth is the capacity for deciding for or against a thing, liberty—*libertas.* The sixth is that choice or a resolution actually taken—*electio.* The seventh is the power of giving the object chosen an existence

—*voluntas.* This seventh power also contains all the others in one figure.

Now the seven powers of the understanding, like the seven powers of our heart and will, can be ennobled and exalted in a very special manner, when we embrace Jesus Christ, as being the wisdom of God, as principle of our reason, and His whole life, which was all love, for motive power of our will.

Our understanding is formed after that of Jesus Christ; First, when we have Him in view in everything, when He forms the only point of sight for all our actions—*intuitus.* Second, when we perceive His actions, His sentiments, and His spirit everywhere—*apperceptio.* Third, when in all our thoughts we reflect upon His sayings, when we think in everything as He would have thought—*reflexio.* Fourth, when we so comfort ourselves in such wise, that His thoughts and His wisdom are the only object for the strength of our imagination—*fantasia.* Fifth, when we reject every thought which would not be His, and when we choose every thought which could be His—*judicium.* Sixth, when in short we co-ordinate the whole edifice of our ideas and spirit upon the model of His ideas and spirit—*ratio.* Seventh, It is then will be born in us a new light, a more brilliant one, surpassing far the light of reason of the senses —*intellectus.* Our heart is also reformed in like manner, when in everything,—First, We lean on

Him only—*desidare.* Second, We wish for Him only—*appetere.* Third, We desire only Him—*concupiscere.* Fourth, We love Him only—*amare.* Fifth, We choose only that which He is, so that we avoid all that He is not—*eligere.* Sixth, We live only in harmony with Him after His commandments and His institutions and orders—*subordinare.* By which in short, Seventh, is born a complete union of our will with His, by which union man is with Jesus Christ but as one sense, one heart; by which perfect union the new man is little by little born in us, and Divine wisdom and love unite to form in us the new spiritual man, in whose heart faith passes into sight, and in comparison to this living faith the treasures of India can be considered but as ashes.

This actual possession of God or Jesus Christ in us is the Centre towards which all the mysteries converge like rays to the circle eye; the highest of the mysteries is this consummation.

The Kingdom of God is a kingdom of truth, morality, and happiness. It operates in the saints from the innermost to the outside, and spreads itself gradually by the Spirit of Jesus Christ into all nations, to institute everywhere an Order by means of which the individual can reach as well as the race; our human nature can be raised to its highest perfection, and sick humanity be cured from all the evils of its weakness.

Thus the love and spirit of God will one day

alone vivify all humanity; they will awake and rekindle all the strength of the human race, will lead it to the goals of Wisdom and place it in suitable relationships.

Peace, fidelity, domestic harmony, love between nations, will be the first fruits of this Spirit. Inspiration of good without false similitudes, the exaltation of our souls without too severe a tension, warmth in the heart without turbulent impatience, will approach, reconcile, and unite all the various parts of the human race, long separated and divided by many differences, and stirred up against each other by prejudices and errors, and in one Grand Temple of Nature, great and little, poor and rich, all will sing the praise of the Father of Love.

Der Baum der Erkenntniß Gutes und Böses.

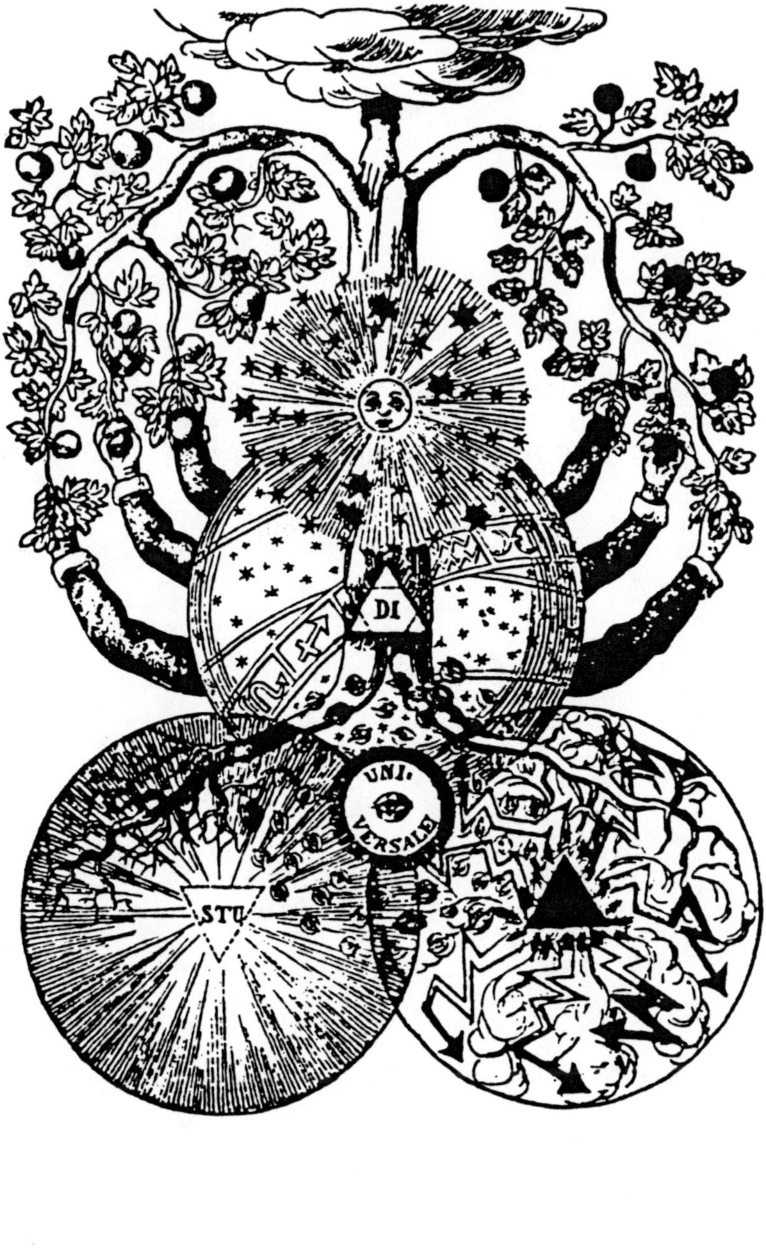

Printed in the United States
124251LV00002B/19/A

9 781585 092772